Packed full of DINO fun!

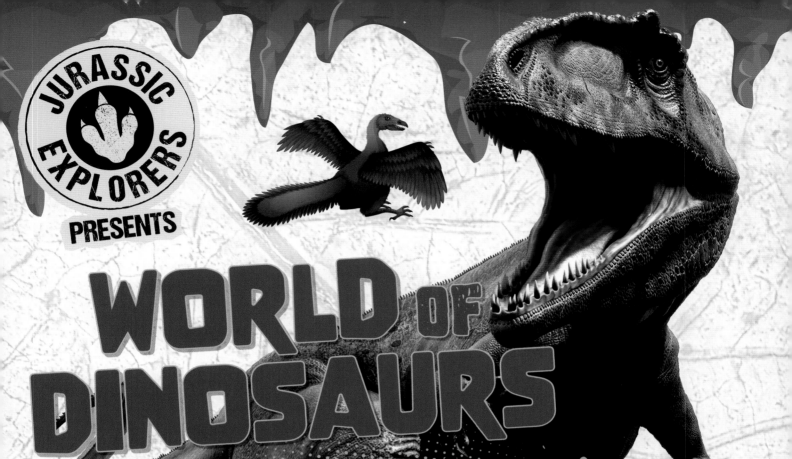

JURASSIC EXPLORERS
PRESENTS

WORLD OF DINOSAURS

THIS BOOK BELONGS TO

_____

_____

Write your name here.

LittleBrother
B O O K S

Published 2022.

Little Brother Books Ltd, Ground Floor,
23 Southernhay East, Exeter, Devon EX1 1QL
books@littlebrotherbooks.co.uk | www.littlebrotherbooks.co.uk

Printed in China. Xuantan Temple Industrial Zone, Gulao Town,
Heshan, Guangdong.

Turn the page
to begin your
Jurassic journey...

DINO IN NEED!

This baby Tyrannosaurus has lost its Dad.
Can you guide it through the maze to find him?

START

Tick a circle as you pass each one.

FINISH

Answers on pages 76-77.

SPOT THE DIFFERENCE

These two pictures may look the same but there are eight dino differences between them.

CAN YOU SPOT THEM ALL?

A

B

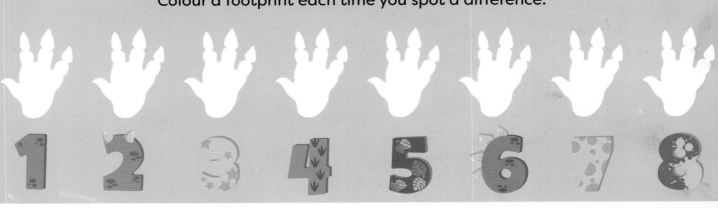

Colour a footprint each time you spot a difference.

1 2 3 4 5 6 7 8

5 FACTS ABOUT...
TYRANNOSAURUS

This fierce predator was the dinosaur king!

DINO STATS

NAME:
TYRANNOSAURUS (TYE-**RAN**-OH-**SORE**-US)

MEANING:
TYRANT LIZARD

FOOD:
MEAT

SIZE:
12M

1 Tyrannosaurus had 60 sharp, long teeth packed inside it's gigantic mouth. The dino's mighty bite was three times as powerful as a lion's and could crush bones.

OUCH!

2 Tyrannosaurus walked on two legs and was a speedy runner. Only the quickest of dinosaurs would have been lucky enough to outrun this giant predator.

3 Tyrannosaurus had a big brain that was twice the size of other giant meat-eaters. T-Rex would have been top of the class at dinosaur school!

4

Although Tyrannosaurus was a gigantic dino, its arms were super small compared to the rest of its body. The reason for T-Rex's little limbs has left scientists baffled.

5

Hungry Tyrannosaurus could swallow small dinosaurs in one giant gulp. That's one way to speed up mealtimes!

WOW!

FOSSIL FIND

Can you spot this Tyrannosaurus fossil hidden somewhere on these pages?

DINO DISCOVERY

Imagine you're an explorer just back from an exciting expedition. Fill in the report below to record what you've seen.

Circle where you went on your expedition.

A forest

The desert

A riverbank

Tick the dinosaurs you spotted.

Parasaurolophus

Tyrannosaurus

Oviraptor

Spinosaurus

Ankylosaurus

Underline what the dinosaurs were doing.

Hunting   **Sleeping**   **Eating**

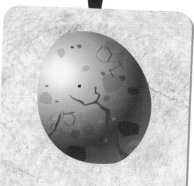

Write how many dinosaur eggs you spotted.

◯

Write how many fossils you found.

◯

Trace over the word that best describes how you felt.

Brave

Excited

Scared

Draw a picture of yourself on the expedition.

5 FACTS ABOUT...
TRICERATOPS

Meet the biggest of the horned dinosaurs.

DINO STATS

NAME:
TRICERATOPS (TRI-**SERRA**-TOPS)

MEANING:
THREE-HORNED FACE

FOOD:
PLANTS

SIZE:
9M

1

The mighty Triceratops was the largest of the horned dinosaurs. With its bulky body, it was as big as an elephant — although much scarier!

2

Triceratops used its three strong horns for fighting or fending off attackers. When Triceratops fought each other, they would bash their heads together.

OUCH!

3

Triceratops had a large, bony frill which it used like a shield to protect its neck from attackers.

4

Inside its beak-like mouth, Triceratops had a whopping 800 teeth. Just think how long a check-up at the dentist would have taken!

MUNCH

5

Hefty Triceratops walked with its toes pointing outwards. Because of its size and weight, it wouldn't have been able to get anywhere in a hurry.

SHADOW MATCH

Circle the shadow that belongs to a Triceratops.

A

B

C

Answers on pages 76-77.

BATTLE ⚡ TIME

How well would dinosaurs fare against some
of the toughest creatures alive today?
Tick your winner for each of these fierce fights.

○ Tyrannosaurus **VS** ○ Lion

○ Allosaurus **VS** ○ Polar Bear

○ Spinosaurus **VS** ○ Crocodile

ODD ONE OUT

Take a good look at these prehistoric pictures. Can you circle the odd one out in each row?

1

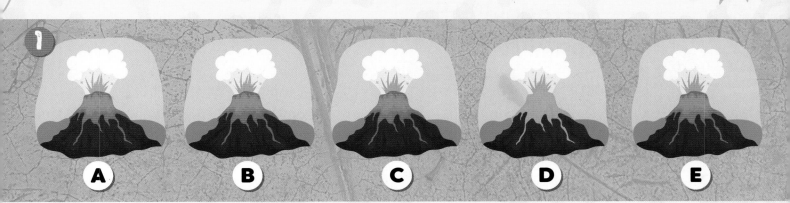

A   B   C   D   E

2

A   B   C   D   E

3

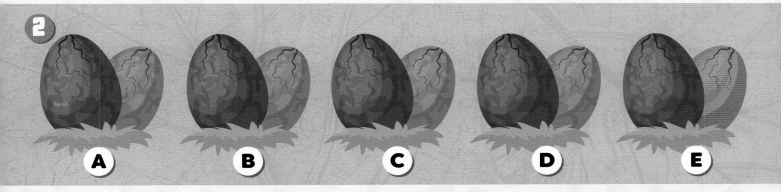

A   B   C   D   E

4

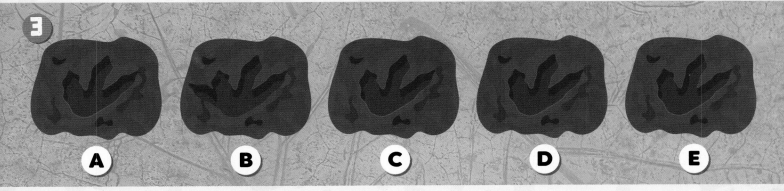

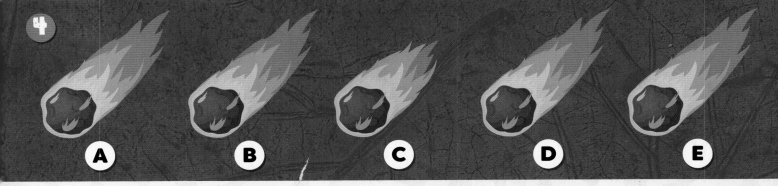

A   B   C   D   E

Answers on pages 76-77.

5 FACTS ABOUT...
DIPLODOCUS

Introducing one of the longest creatures to ever walk the Earth.

DINO STATS

NAME:
DIPLODOCUS (DIP-LOW **DOCK**-US)

MEANING:
DOUBLE BEAM

FOOD:
PLANTS

SIZE:
27M

1 With its supersized tail and neck, Diplodocus was as long as a blue whale.

WOW!

2 Diplodocus used its long tail to frighten away predators. When whipped, it made a loud booming sound.

SCARY!

TRUE OR FALSE?

Diplodocus was as long as a shark? Circle the right answer.

TRUE   **FALSE**

3

As well as feasting on leaves, Diplodocus also swallowed stones. They helped the dinosaur to digest the tough plants it had eaten.

YUCK!

4

Diplodocus lived in the USA 155-145 million years ago. It is the longest dinosaur for which a complete skeleton has been discovered.

5

Although lots of images show Diplodocus holding its head up high, some scientists don't believe this would have been possible because the dino's heart couldn't have pumped blood that far upwards.

Answers on pages 76-77.

AWARD WINNERS

BIGGEST PREDATOR

At 16m long, the gigantic Spinosaurus was the biggest meat-eater to ever walk the Earth.

SMALLEST BRAIN

When it comes to comparing the size of a dinosaur to the size of its brain, there can only be one winner – Stegosaurus. This 9m long dino had a tiny brain the size of an apple.

SMALLEST

At 40cm long, the bird-like Anchiornis was about the size of a magpie.

HEAVIEST

Experts have estimated that Agentinosaurus weighed as much as 20 elephants! It would have taken a lot of leaves for this plant-eater to maintain that mind-blowing weight!

FASTEST

It's estimated that the ostrich-like Gallimimus could run as quickly as 50mph – fast enough to beat a racehorse in a race.

WOW!

TALLEST

With its long legs and neck, Sauroposeidon reached heights of 18m – that's as tall as a six storey building.

THICKEST SKULL

Pachycephalosaurus had a skull 20 times thicker than other dinosaurs. It may have used its hard head to fight off dinos that got too close.

LONGEST

With its supersized neck and tail, Diplodocus could stretch to over 50m long – that's the length of two swimming pools.

LONGEST CLAW

The award for longest claw goes to Therizinosaurus. Its scary talons were a whopping 91cm – that's as long as a man's arm!

5 FACTS ABOUT...
IGUANODON

Meet the heavy dinosaur with a built-in weapon.

DINO STATS

NAME:
IGUANODON (IG-WHA-NOH-DON)

MEANING:
IGUANA TOOTH

FOOD:
PLANTS

SIZE:
9M

1

Heavy Iguanodon weighed nearly as much as two cars. It had super strong leg bones to support its bulky body.

2

Iguanodon was one of the first ever dinosaurs to be identified after fossils of its teeth were discovered in Sussex, England, 200 years ago.

WOW!

3

Iguanodon had a thumb spike on its hand which would have been used like a weapon to fend of predators.

OUCH!

UP CLOSE

Which of these close-ups isn't from Iguanodon?

A

B

C

4

Iguanodon had curved and grooved teeth. They were helpful for grinding the tough plants which grew at that time.

5

When Iguanodon was first discovered, scientists wrongly thought that its thumb spike was a horn from its head.

OOPS!

Answers on pages 76-77.

23

BALLOON DINO

YOU WILL NEED

A green balloon

Thick green paper

Pencil

Scissors

Double-sided sticky tape

Glue

2 googly eyes

You don't need much to make this roar-some balloon Stegosaurus.

HOW TO MAKE

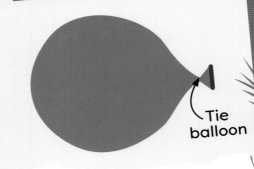
— Tie balloon

1 Blow up the balloon and tie a knot in the end.

Adult guidance is needed for this activity.

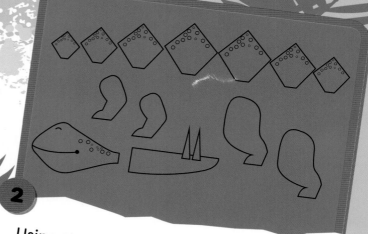

2 Using the picture of the finished balloon dinosaur to help you, draw the following dinosaur body parts onto the green paper – head, two front legs, two back legs, seven pentagon-shaped back plates, and a tail.

3 Draw a tab – about 1cm wide – onto each body part, where it will be attached to the balloon.

Draw tab

4 Carefully cut out the body parts and fold back the tabs.

Careful!

5 Stick a piece of double-sided sticky tape onto each tab and attach the body parts to the balloon.

Double sided tape

6 Glue a googly eye onto each side of the head and your balloon Stegosaurus is complete.

5 FACTS ABOUT...
VELOCIRAPTOR

This feathered dinosaur was fast on its feet.

DINO STATS

NAME:
VELOCIRAPTOR (VEL-**OSS**-EE-RAP-TOR)

MEANING:
SPEED THIEF

FOOD:
MEAT

SIZE:
2M

1

Velociraptor was only about the size of a large dog. It may have been small, but that didn't make it any less deadly!

2

Velociraptor was super speedy and could run as fast as a tiger. It used its long, stiff tail to keep balance as it ran.

3

Vicious Velociraptor had a mouth full of razor-sharp teeth and three pointed claws on each hand and foot.

4 Velociraptors hunted in packs. They used their sharp claws to grip and slash any creature unlucky enough to be caught.

OUCH!

5 Velociraptor was a meat-eater and feasted on small lizards, mammals and dinosaur eggs. Experts think it probably gobbled up baby dinos too.

EGG HUNT

How many dinosaur eggs can you find hidden on these pages?

DINO DETECTIVE

Use the clues to work out which of the dinosaurs below has eaten the most leaves on the tree.

CLUE 1
It doesn't have a neck frill.

CLUE 2
It doesn't have back plates.

CLUE 3
It doesn't have a head crest.

CLUE 4
It has a long neck.

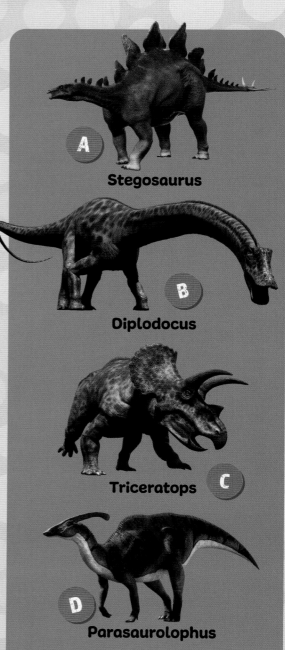

A — Stegosaurus

B — Diplodocus

C — Triceratops

D — Parasaurolophus

....

has eaten the most leaves.

Answers on pages 76-77.

FOSSIL FIND

Imagine you're a scientist off to find dinosaur fossils. Finish the crossword to find out what you need to pack in your tool kit.

brush

chisel

trowel

hammer

5 FACTS ABOUT...
ALLOSAURUS

This deadly dino was a fierce predator.

DINO STATS

NAME:
ALLOSAURUS (AL-OH-**SAW**-RUSS)

MEANING:
OTHER LIZARD

FOOD:
MEAT

SIZE:
12M

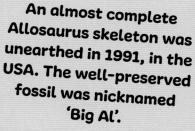

1
Fearsome Allosaurus lived in Portugal and the USA 156–144 million years ago. This giant meat-eater was the king of the North American Jurassic predators.

2
Allosaurus had 70 dagger-like teeth that curved backwards to stop its prey from escaping.

COOL!

3
An almost complete Allosaurus skeleton was unearthed in 1991, in the USA. The well-preserved fossil was nicknamed 'Big Al'.

4

Allosaurus could make its mouth bigger to fit in huge chunks of meat. The deadly dino could bend its lower jawbones outwards when it needed to make more room.

AWESOME!

5

Allosaurus liked to hunt alone rather than in a pack. Fossils have shown that those hunting together often ended up attacking each other!

FOOTPRINT FUN

Which Allosaurus footprint is the odd one out?

A   B   C   D

Answers on pages 76-77.

ESCAPE ROUTE

These plant-eaters need to escape from the hungry T-Rex!

A Ankylosaurus

B Apatosaurus

C Iguanodon

Colour each trail a different colour and count how many footprints will lead each dino to safety.

footprints

footprints

footprints

Answers on pages 76-77.

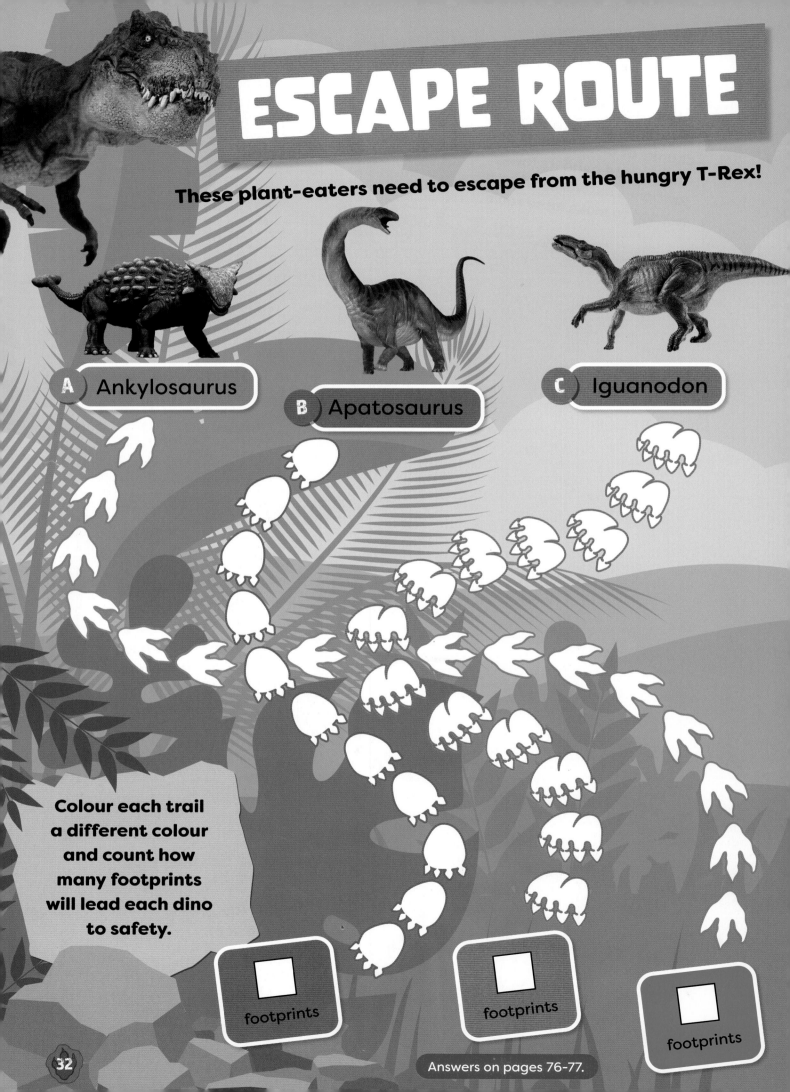

QUICK QUIZ

Tick true or false to answer each question.

Test your dino knowledge with this fun quiz. All of the answers can be found somewhere in this book.

1 Tyrannosaurus was a plant-eater.

TRUE ⬜ FALSE ⬜

2 Spinosaurus could swim.

TRUE ⬜ FALSE ⬜

3 Diplodocus was as long as a blue whale.

TRUE ⬜ FALSE ⬜

4 Microraptor was the biggest meat-eater.

TRUE ⬜ FALSE ⬜

5 Stegosaurus didn't have any teeth.

TRUE ⬜ FALSE ⬜

Answers on pages 76-77.

PREHISTORIC PICTURE

Follow the instructions to add your own dinosaur doodles to this picture.

Draw some leaves for this hungry Stegosaurus.

Make the volcano erupt by adding some lava.

Add another fossil to this collection.

Draw some eggs in the dinosaur nest.

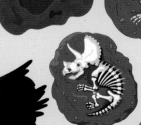

APATOSAURUS

This tall dinosaur had a very noisy tail.

DINO STATS

NAME:
APATOSAURUS (AH-**PAT**-OH-SORE-US)

MEANING:
DECEPTIVE LIZARD

FOOD:
PLANTS

SIZE:
21M

1

Apatosaurus had a looooong tail. It helped the huge dino balance and could also be cracked like a whip to scare off attackers. An Apatosaurus tail made a louder sound than a cannon.

BOOM!

2

When it was searching for food, plant-eating Apatosaurus used its strong, flexible neck to knock down trees, just like elephants do today.

4

Apatosaurus had spoon-shaped teeth. Like some other plant-eaters, it swallowed stones to help grind up the food inside its stomach.

3

The gigantic Apatosaurus laid supersized eggs that were are big as a basketball. Imagine trying to fit that in your frying pan!

WOW!

5

Apatosaurus lived in herds. They may have migrated, like many animals living today do.

WHERE IN THE WORLD?

Where did Apatosaurus live? Copy the letters into the matching coloured circles to reveal the country.

A U S

Answers on pages 76-77.

BEAT THE CLOCK

Can you match these dinosaurs into pairs in less than two minutes? Ready, steady, go!

Allosaurus

Triceratops

Coelophysis

Velociraptor

Parasaurolophus

Brachiosaurus

Tyrannosaurus Rex

Spinosaurus

Stegosaurus

Ankylosaurus

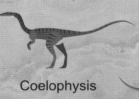

Brachiosaurus

Coelophysis

Spinosaurus

Stegosaurus

Parasaurolophus

Allosaurus

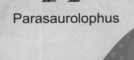

Triceratops

Tyrannosaurus Rex

Ankylosaurus

HOW LONG DID IT TAKE?

Colour the stopwatch if you smashed the two minute challenge.

Less than 30 seconds = colour the stopwatch **red**

30 seconds to 1 minute = colour the stopwatch **blue**

More than 1 minute = colour the stopwatch **green**

Answers on pages 76-77.

STEGOSAURUS

This large dinosaur was very slow-moving.

DINO STATS

NAME:
STEGOSAURUS (**STEG**-OH-**SORE**-US)

MEANING:
ROOF LIZARD

FOOD:
PLANTS

SIZE:
9M

1

A fully grown Stegosaurus was as long as a bus. This giant beast was the biggest of the plate-backed plant-eating dinosaurs.

WOW!

2

Stegosaurus used its strong tail as a weapon to fend of attackers. It could be swung from side-to-side and had a spike on the end that could be as long as 1m.

3

Bulky Stegosaurus may have been the size of an elephant, but it had a tiny brain. Experts believe it was only as big as a walnut.

4

Some scientists think that Stegosaurus' back plates may have been able to turn red to scare off attackers. How cool is that?

COOL!

5

Plant-eating Stegosaurus was a toothless dino. Instead of chewing its food, it had a sharp beak which it used to nibble plants.

HEADING HOME

Which path will lead this sleepy Stegosaurus back to its cave?

C

B

A

Answers on pages 76-77.

MAKE AND WEAR

Dress up as a dinosaur with this cool spiky headdress – you'll look roar-some!

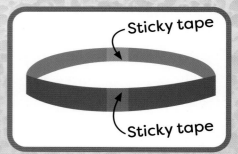

Adult guidance is needed for this activity.

YOU WILL NEED

3 A4 sheets of thin green paper

Pencil

Ruler

Scissors

Sticky tape

Glue

HOW TO MAKE

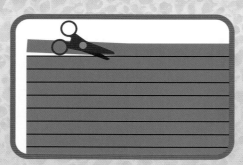

1 Take one sheet of green paper and draw lines to divide it into seven 3cm wide strips, along the long side of the sheet. Cut the strips out.

2 Use sticky tape to join two of the strips together, end to end, to make one long strip. Then join the ends of the long strip together to make a band big enough to fit around your head.

Sticky tape

Sticky tape

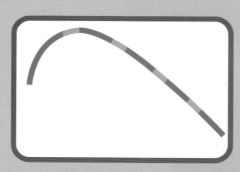

3 Stick the remaining five strips together to form one long strip. This is the cross piece that you will stick your spikes onto. If the length is too long for your height, just snip a bit off the end.

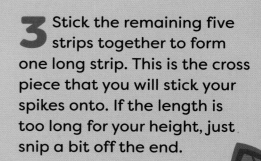

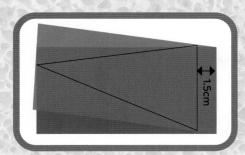

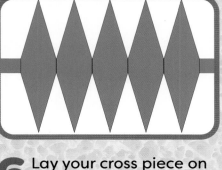

4 Take the other two sheets of green paper and draw lines to divide them into 5cm wide strips, along the long side. Cut the strips out. These will make your spikes.

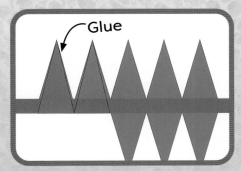

5 Fold a spike strip in half, then draw a triangle on it, starting 1.5cm above the folded edge, as shown in the picture. When opened out your spike will look a bit like a diamond. Repeat this step for all of your spike strips.

1.5cm

6 Lay your cross piece on a flat surface and glue the open spikes along the length of it.

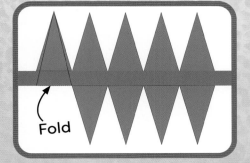

Fold

7 Turn the cross piece over so that the spikes are on the bottom. Fold each side of each spike over the central strip to create a crease.

Glue

8 Glue the two sides of the top spike together to create one triangle shaped spike. Repeat this step for all of the spikes. Leave your cross piece until the glue is completely dry.

9 Use sticky tape to attach the spiked cross piece to the headband. Your spiky dinosaur headdress is now ready to wear. ROAR!

SPINOSAURUS

This huge dino had an eye-catching sail.

DINO STATS

NAME:
SPINOSAURUS (**SPINE**-OH-**SORE**-US)

MEANING:
THORN LIZARD

FOOD:
MEAT AND FISH

SIZE:
16M

1
Spinosaurus holds the title of longest meat-eating dinosaur. This gigantic beast may have reached lengths of 15m — that's as long as four small cars parked bumper-to-bumper.

WOW!

2
Fish was always on the menu for this swampland dinosaur. It had webbed feet, like a duck, which helped it walk along riverbeds to catch its prey.

3
Spinosaurus had a huge sail on its back but experts don't really know what it was for. It could have been used to store up energy or to help the dinosaur stay underwater.

COOL!

4

Spinosaurus had long jaws, similar to a crocodile's, and sharp teeth. It also had high-up nostrils to make it easier to breath in water.

5

Only small parts of tail fossils have ever been found, so scientists don't know for certain what Spinosaurus' tail actually looked like.

FAMILY FUN

Can you put this Spinosaurus family in order of size, starting with the smallest?

A

B

C

Answers on pages 76-77.

DANGER ALERT

Watch out, deadly dinos about! Give each of these prehistoric predators a danger rating on the danger-meter.

DANGEROUS DINO

FIERCE FIGHTER

DOESN'T SCARE ME

ANKYLOSAURUS

(AN-KIE-LOH-SORE-US)

This tough dinosaur used its dangerous tail to whack attackers.

SUCHOMIMUS

(SOO-KO-MIME-US)

With over 120 teeth, this crocodile-like predator was not to be messed with!

GIGANOTOSAURUS

(GIG-AN-OH-TOE-SORE-US)

A fierce meat-eater with an excellent sense of smell for sniffing out prey.

CARCHARODONTOSAURUS

(CAR-CARE-OH-DON-TOE-SORE-US)

This bulky giant could cause some serious damage with its shark-like teeth.

COLOURING TIME

Use your favourite crayons or pens to add some roar-some colours to this hungry Triceratops.

5 FACTS ABOUT...

ANKYLOSAURUS

This bulky dino was as tough as they came.

DINO STATS

NAME:
ANKYLOSAURUS (AN-**KIE**-LOH-SORE-US)

MEANING:
STIFF LIZARD

FOOD:
PLANTS

SIZE:
10M

1
Ankylosaurus was built like a tank. Unusually for a dinosaur, its body was wider than it was tall.

2
Thick plates, spikes and studs covered Ankylosaurus like body armour, making it hard for other dinosaurs to attack. Even its eyelids were covered in small, bony plates.

COOL!

3

Although it was slow-moving, Ankylosaurus was still a deadly dino. It had a bony club on the end of its tail for attacking any predator that dared to get close.

THUMP!

4

Inside its horny beak, Ankylosaurus had small, leaf-shaped teeth. These gnashers were perfect for snipping plants.

5

Ankylosaurus lived in Canada and the USA 74-67 million years ago, during the Cretaceous time period.

PLANT PATTERN

What comes next in this sequence? Colour the white leaf the correct colour.

Answers on pages 76-77.

DINOSAUR HUNT

Mini Microraptors are hard to spot! Can you find all 10 hiding in this prehistoric forest?

DID YOU KNOW?
Microraptor was only 40cm long.

Tick a circle as you spot each Microraptor.

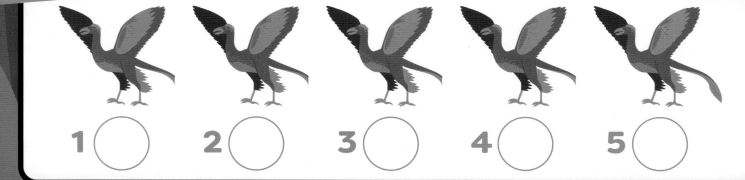

1 ○   2 ○   3 ○   4 ○   5 ○

6 ◯ 7 ◯ 8 ◯ 9 ◯ 10 ◯

5 FACTS ABOUT...
MICRORAPTOR

The long feathers on its arms and legs made this tiny dino a clumsy runner!

DINO STATS

NAME:
MICRORAPTOR (**MIKE**-ROW-RAP-TOR)

MEANING:
SMALL THIEF

FOOD:
MEAT

SIZE:
40CM

1

Only about the size of a seagull, tiny Microraptor was one of the smallest meat-eating dinosaurs.

2

Microraptor had feathered wings, like a bird, but it couldn't fly. Instead it glided from tree to tree.

3

Meat-eating Microraptor ate small animals and insects. It caught its prey with its sharp teeth and claws.

WHEEEE!

OUCH!

4

Microraptor spent most of its times in trees, hunting prey. Its ability to glide helped the bird-like dino to quickly escape from predators.

COOL!

5

Microraptor had a fan of feathers at the end of its long tail. Experts believe this may have helped the dinosaur to keep its balance in the air.

DINO DINNER

Microraptor is hunting for food. How many insects can you count in this jumble?

Answers on pages 76-77.

FOSSIL FUN

Will you be the first to collect all five fossils in this exciting dinosaur game?

START

YOU WILL NEED

A dice

2 counters

2 crayons

1 Decide who will be player 1 and who will be player 2.

2 Take it in turns to roll the dice and move your counter around the board.

3 If you land on a fossil, colour one of the fossils on your player card.

4 Keep moving around the board until one player has coloured all five of their fossils – they are the winner.

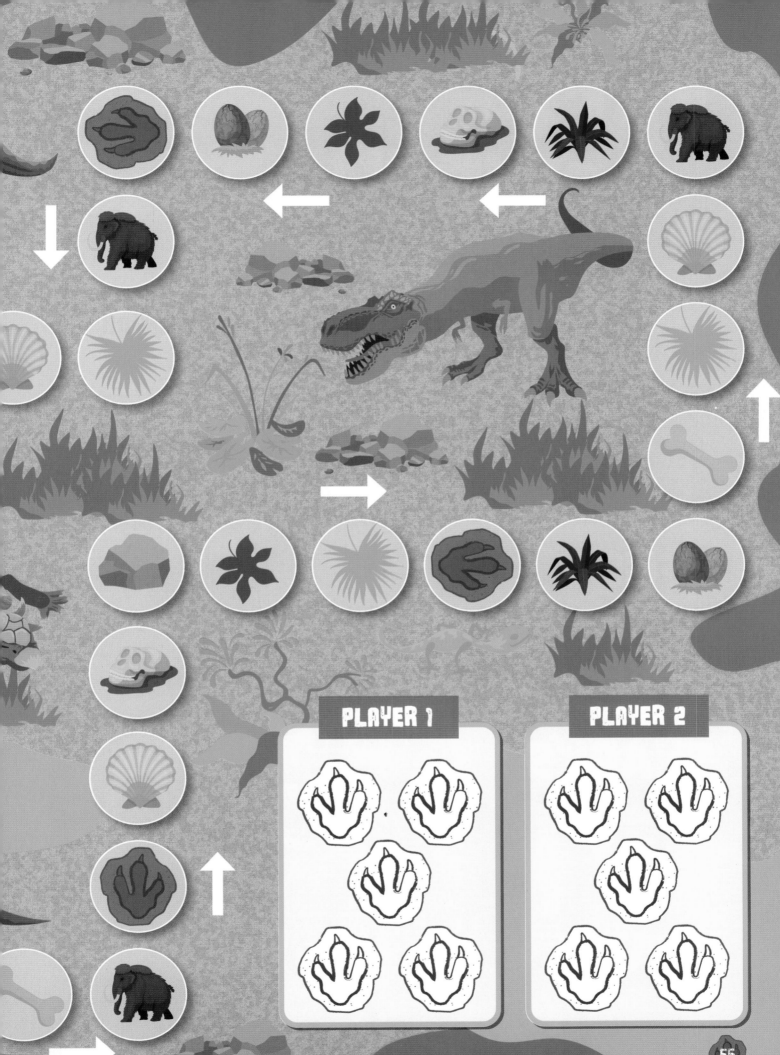

PLAYER 1

PLAYER 2

55

FACT FINDER

Fill in the gaps to complete these facts, by choosing the right word from the volcano.

1 DINOSAURS COULDN'T SWIM OR

_____

FOOD

SMALL

SHARKS

FLY

TAILS

2 THE WORLD'S FIRST DINOSAURS WERE ALL

_____

3 ALL DINOSAURS HAD

_____

TO HELP THEM BALANCE.

4 DINOSAURS USED THEIR CLAWS FOR GATHERING

_____

5 _____

EXISTED BEFORE DINOSAURS.

Answers on pages 76-77.

PARASAUROLOPHUS

Meet the dinosaur that could make music!

DINO STATS

NAME:
PARASAUROLOPHUS (PA-RA-SAW-**ROL**-OFF-US)

MEANING:
NEAR CRESTED LIZARD

FOOD:
PLANTS

SIZE:
9M

1

Unusual looking Parasaurolophus was a duckbill dinosaur. Its wide, flat mouth looked a bit like a duck's beak.

2

Parasaurolophus had a crest on its head that could make a sound like a trumpet. This might have been how Parasaurolophus talked to other dinosaurs.

3

Inside its beak-like mouth, plant-eating Parasaurolophus had hundreds of tiny teeth. These may have been used to grind up tough leaves.

CHOMP!

4

Parasaurolophus could walk on two or four legs. Its back legs were super strong — perfect for standing on to reach high-up leaves.

WOW!

5

Parasaurolophus lived in the woodlands of Canada and the USA. They travelled in large herds.

DINO DIFFERENCES

Can you spot three differences between these Parasaurolophus fossils?

Answers on pages 76-77.

HIDDEN FACTS

Crack the code to discover some fascinating facts about Dilophosaurus.

KEY

A	B	C	D	E	F	G	H	I	J	K	L	M

N	O	P	Q	R	S	T	U	V	W	X	Y	Z

1 Dilophosaurus was a

F A S I

runner.

2 Dilophosaurus had two bony

C R E S T S

on its head.

3 Dilophosaurus had a

J A W

similar to a crocodile's.

Answers on pages 76-77.

TRAIL TWIST

Count the number of dinos in each herd, then follow the twisting trails to write your answers in the correct boxes.

1

2

3

4

5

Answers on pages 76-77.

5 FACTS ABOUT...

GIGANOTOSAURUS

This South American dino was gigantic and deadly.

DINO STATS

NAME:
GIGANOTOSAURUS (GIG-AN-**OH**-TOE-**SORE**-US)

MEANING:
GIANT SOUTHERN LIZARD

FOOD:
MEAT

SIZE:
12M

1

Deadly Giganotosaurus was one of the world's largest dinosaurs. Some experts believe it was bigger and heavier than Tyrannosaurus.

WOW!

2

Giganotosaurus lived in Argentina 112-90 million years ago. Scientists think these supersized dinos travelled in groups made up of dinosaurs of all ages.

3

Although it was massive, Giganotosaurus had a small brain for its size, about as big as a cucumber.

FANCY THAT!

4

The only evidence that's been found of Giganotosaurus so far is one almost complete skeleton and a piece of jawbone.

5

Meat-eating Giganotosaurus had long, blade-like teeth. These sharp gnashers would have been perfect for slicing flesh.

OUCH!

DINO COLOURING

Add some fierce colours to this roaring Giganotosaurus.

ERUPTING VOLCANO

You'll have so much fun making this volcano explode! Boom!

Adult guidance is needed for this activity.

YOU WILL NEED

500ml empty plastic bottle

Scissors

2 sheets of brown foam

Glue

Baking tray

FOR THE EXPLOSION

Bicarbonate of soda

Vinegar

Teaspoon

Jug of warm water

Red food colouring

HOW TO MAKE

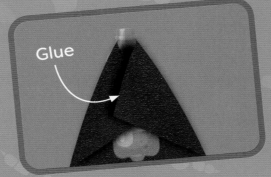
Glue

1 Wrap a piece of brown foam around the rim of the bottle to make a cone shape and glue it in place.

2 Glue the other piece of foam around the other side so that the bottle is completely covered. Trim any excess foam from the bottom so that the bottle will stand up.

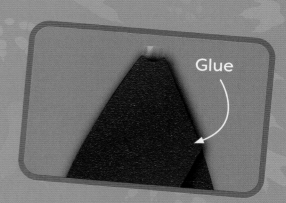
Glue

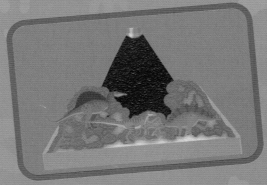

3 Place your bottle on a baking tray. You can decorate the base with sand or moss and toy dinosaurs if you want.

4 In a jug, add 450ml of warm water, a few drops of red food colouring and four heaped teaspoons of bicarbonate of soda. Mix everything well then pour the red liquid into the bottle.

450ml →

TOP TIP

Pour the vinegar quickly before the bicarbonate of soda settles to the bottom of the water. If your volcano doesn't erupt, you need to add more vinegar.

5 Now for the fun bit! Quickly pour a big squirt of vinegar into the bottle and watch your volcano erupt.

5 FACTS ABOUT...
OVIRAPTOR

Introducing the desert dinosaur from China and Mongolia.

DINO FACTFILE

NAME:
OVIRAPTOR (OH-VEE-RAP-TOR)

MEANING:
EGG THIEF

FOOD:
MEAT AND PLANTS

SIZE:
2.4M

1

Oviraptor laid its eggs in a spiral pattern. Fossils have shown that it sat on top of them, like many birds to today.

2

Unusually for a meat-eater, Oviraptor was a toothless dino. Instead of chewing, it may have swallowed its prey whole. Luckily it only ate small animals!

GULP!

3

Oviraptor was given the name 'egg thief' because an explorer once thought it stole eggs from other dinosaurs. A fossil uncovered nearly 70 years later showed that this wasn't true.

4

Oviraptor had a beak-like mouth. Its curved jaw help it crush hard objects.

COOL!

5

Some experts believe that Oviraptor had feathered wings. These may have been used to protect and shelter their young in the nest.

QUESTION TIME

How many legs did Oviraptor walk on? Trace over the word below to write the answer.

two

DINO FIGHT

DID YOU KNOW?
Fearsome Suchomimus was as big as a T-Rex.

Spikes along back and tail.

Over 120 sharp teeth.

Powerful body.

DID YOU KNOW?
Suchomimus ate fish and marine reptiles. Its teeth pointed backwards so it could keep hold of its slippery prey.

Sharp claws.

Suchomimus Scores	
Size	/10
Strength	/10
Speed	/10
Fierceness	/10
TOTAL	/40

SUCHOMIMUS

NAME: SUCHOMIMUS (**SOO**-KO-**MIME**-US) **MEANING:** CROCODILE MIMIC **FOOD:** MEAT **SIZE:** 9M

DID YOU KNOW? Fierce Utahraptor weighed as much as a polar bear.

Which of these two mighty meat-eaters would win in a battle? Give each dinosaur marks out of 10 to choose the champion.

Lots of sharp, pointed teeth.

Powerful legs for fast running.

DID YOU KNOW? Utahraptor used its deadly toe claw to slash and stab its prey.

Utahraptor Scores	
Size	/10
Strength	/10
Speed	/10
Fierceness	/10
TOTAL	/40

Hooked claws.

Huge toe claw.

VS UTAHRAPTOR

NAME: UTAHRAPTOR (**YOU**-TAH-**RAP**-TOR) **MEANING:** UTAH PLUNDERER **FOOD:** MEAT **SIZE:** 7M

THE WINNER IS ....

DINOSAUR
WANNABES!

These prehistoric flying reptiles and sea creatures are often mistaken for dinosaurs, but no dinosaur could actually fly or swim.

PTERANODON
(TE-RAN-O-DON)

Pteranodon was one of the biggest flying creatures ever. Its name means 'wings and no teeth'. It lived in huge flocks and flew over the sea looking for fish to catch in its long beak.

KRONOSAURUS
(CRONE-OH-SORE-US)

Kronosaurus was one of the largest sea reptiles. This gigantic creature was as long as a bus and its head alone was bigger than a person! It lived in the Australian seas around 100 million years ago.

PLESIOSAURUS
(PLE-SEE-OH-SORE-US)

Plesiosaurus was a large, swimming reptile. It had sharp teeth, a long neck, a broad body and flippers, like a whale. Many Plesiosaurus fossils have been found along the coastlines of the UK.

DIMETRODON
(DIE-MEE-TRO-DON)

Dimetrodon lived about 275 million years ago, before dinosaurs even existed. It walked on four legs and had a large, eye-catching sail. Dimetrodon had teeth hidden on the roof of its mouth so it could easily keep hold of its prey.

COOL!

FISHY FUN

Can you match these fish into pairs before Plesiosaurus eats them up?

A
B
C
D
E
F
G
H

Answers on pages 76-77.

MAKE A MATCH

How quickly can you match these roaring dinosaurs to their shadows? 3... 2... 1... go!

Answers on pages 76-77.

DINO WARS

Will you win the dinosaur war in this fast and fierce card game for three players?

TURN THE PAGE TO FIND OUT HOW TO PLAY.

TYRANNOSAURUS

LENGTH IN METRES:	12
AGE: (MILLIONS OF YEARS)	67
FIERCE RATING:	10

STEGOSAURUS

LENGTH IN METRES:	9
AGE: (MILLIONS OF YEARS)	156
FIERCE RATING:	2

DIPLODOCUS

LENGTH IN METRES:	27
AGE: (MILLIONS OF YEARS)	155
FIERCE RATING:	0

GIGANOTOSAURUS

LENGTH IN METRES:	12
AGE: (MILLIONS OF YEARS)	112
FIERCE RATING:	10

TRICERATOPS

LENGTH IN METRES:	9
AGE: (MILLIONS OF YEARS)	68
FIERCE RATING:	4

VELOCIRAPTOR

LENGTH IN METRES:	2
AGE: (MILLIONS OF YEARS)	74
FIERCE RATING:	9

SPINOSAURUS

LENGTH IN METRES:	16
AGE: (MILLIONS OF YEARS)	95
FIERCE RATING:	10

ANKYLOSAURUS

LENGTH IN METRES:	10
AGE: (MILLIONS OF YEARS)	74
FIERCE RATING:	5

MICRORAPTOR

LENGTH IN METRES:	0.4
AGE: (MILLIONS OF YEARS)	125
FIERCE RATING:	1

HOW TO PLAY

1 Carefully cut out the cards along the dotted lines.

2 Shuffle the cards and deal them out equally between three players. Place your cards face down in a pile.

3 Each player takes the top card from their pile. The youngest player goes first by choosing the first category.

4 Whoever has the highest rating in that category wins all of the cards and chooses the next category. If the ratings are the same, all the cards are placed in the middle and whoever wins the next round wins those cards too.

5 Keep playing with the top card on your piles until one player has won all the cards – they are the Dino Wars champion.

DOTTY DRAWING

Join the dots to finish this picture of the musical Parasaurolophus, then add some cool colours.

What sound could Parasaurolophus make with its head crest?

NEED HELP? You can find the fo...

ANSWERS

PAGES 6-7
DINO IN NEED!

PAGES 8-9
SPOT THE DIFFERENCE

PAGES 14-15
SHADOW MATCH
B.

PAGE 17
ODD ONE OUT
1. D.
2. E.
3. B.
4. C.

PAGES 18-19
TRUE OR FALSE?
False – Diplodocus was as long as a blue whale.

PAGES 22-23
UP CLOSE
A.

PAGES 26-27
EGG HUNT
6 eggs.

PAGE 28
DINO DETECTIVE
Diplodocus has eaten the most leaves.

PAGE 29
FOSSIL FIND

PAGES 30-31
FOOTPRINT FUN
C.

PAGE 32
ESCAPE ROUTE
Ankylosaurus – 15, Apatosaurus – 11, Iguanodon – 13.